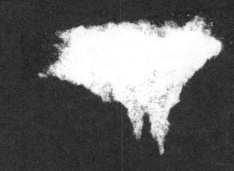

Tigger 1989
Syon Park

The *Essential* CAT

The *Essential* CAT

Paddy Cutts

Brian Trodd Publishing House Limited

Published in 1991 by
Brian Trodd Publishing House Limited
27 Swinton Street, London WC1X 9NW

Copyright © 1991 Brian Trodd Publishing House Limited

ISBN 1 85361 215 4
Printed in Portugal

Acknowledgments

My grateful thanks to the following beings, human and feline,
who have helped me compile this book:

Cutlet, Arfur and Trotter (my cats) who have added their own
little passages to the manuscript! They love playing with the
word processor, and also think that one of their most important
tasks is to keep my light box warm – preferably by sitting on it!

Daphne Negus (Cat World International) for her helpful
comments on the Anglo-American aspects of cat ownership, and
for her very kind, and most flattering preface.

Chris Collier and Linda Burroughs, the two editors who have
made my job just that much easier.

Sal Marsh and Rosemary Alger for helping me to put my
thoughts onto the word processor, and for adding their own
amusing feline anecdotes.

Murray Thomas for his patience in showing me how to use the
word processor more efficiently and effectively, and for his
general moral support to me while I was working under pressure!

Colour Centre for processing my films with their usual care and
efficiency.

Last but not least, to the beautiful cats it has been my privilege
to photograph over the years, and to their kind owners for giving
me their permission so to do. Without you, there would be no
book!

CONTENTS

PREFACE

Multi-talented photographer Paddy Cutts has conveyed the beauty of cats the world over. Here, author Paddy Cutts shares the joys of cat companionship in words as well. Airing my lifelong affinity with the feline race in Paddy's book is a pleasure indeed.

No cat can be expected to conform to any preconceived idea of how a cat behaves. Each is distinctly memorable. Not everyone likes cats. Not every cat likes other cats. A lot of cats are brighter than a lot of people. Some cats don't like people in general but will bond to one person. Some just don't like people at all. Only a few are actually independent. Usually, a cat responds in kind to the depth of love extended to it by a human. Wherever it is regarded merely as non-essential it may seem to exist in an independent mode, but is just keeping its feelings stored away until somebody loving comes along. If that doesn't happen, the cat will make the best of life as it comes. Cats don't squander anything.

There are cats who may well cruise the neighborhood in search of warmer relationships, human and feline. Roaming cats are at grave risk in most neighborhoods – unwelcome in other people's gardens, liable to be killed by enemies, stolen for nefarious purposes, deliberately or inadvertently poisoned, and vulnerable to disease and fight injuries. Paddy has good reason to advocate safe keeping practices to those who still think cats must have unlimited freedom.

A great understanding of cats and how essential they are is conveyed in this book, with Paddy's lovely photos on view to illustrate how everyone can contribute to the happy life for every cat.

Daphne Negus
Editrix/co-Publisher
CAT WORLD INTERNATIONAL

INTRODUCTION

The brief was to write a "different" cat book; not the usual guide to cat and kitten care, or an encyclopedia of the various breeds, or even how to photograph them, but something that would catch the "essence" of that most popular of domestic pets, the cat. Although, at first, this seemed to be a somewhat daunting task, the more I became involved in the project the more interesting it became. It really made me look long and hard at my photographs; why is the cat doing that, what is it thinking, how on earth did it get up there? All of these questions came to mind, making me realize that there is an awful lot that we will never fully understand about the felines we choose to share our lives with, but we can at least try!

Cats can come in all sorts of shapes and sizes, with different lengths, colors, and patterns of fur, but most importantly each and every one has its own distinctive personality. Even within one litter there will be considerable differences between the siblings. Even at a tender age, their characters will be evident; some will be bossy, some timid, and others extrovert, but few will be shy of humans if they have been brought up in a domestic environment and handled from birth.

I cannot remember a time when cats did not feature in my life. For the last 20 years I have shared my home with Burmese cats, the three that I have now being descendants of my original queen. They are all happy, contented neuters of "pensionable" age, but are still as active as they were when kittens! Through my photography, I have been invited into many cat-loving homes where I have been able to see, at first hand, just how different cats can be, not just in appearance but also in behavior. This has given me a privileged insight into the secret world of so many cats, whereas most people only really get to know   their own cats, or those of their friends and neighbors.

Although, in the main, this book is light hearted, it also tries to give good, sensible advice, which I hope will not fall on deaf ears. Cats have the reputation of being independent and self-sufficient, and in their natural habitat, they can be. In an urban environment, domesticated by humans, it is up to us to take the responsibility for their continued welfare.

It has given me tremendous pleasure to write this book; I hope that you enjoy reading it, and that it will give just a little bit more insight into the world of the wild animal that we have tamed to live with us in our homes.

A DAY IN THE LIFE OF A CAT

The way that we acquire cats, or perhaps more often they acquire us, is often curious. This cat did a real "hard sell" on his prospective new owner as, when she was looking for a house to buy, he managed to position himself quite obviously in front of the house when the photograph to accompany the sale details was being taken. The house-hunter knew that this had to be the house for her – it came with a cat (this, despite the fact that she already owned nearly a dozen Siamese cats!).

True to feline persuasiveness, the cat was in the garden the day she went to view the property. Of course, she bought the house! After moving in, she didn't see the cat for some considerable time. Returning from work on a wet and windy night, she saw that he had taken up residence in an unused dog kennel. She felt that he might like some supper, and so started feeding him. Start feeding a cat, and you have a friend for life!

As it turned out, the cat belonged to the next-door neighbor, who was not really cat oriented. The cat had turned up on his doorstep and, although he didn't really like cats, would never be

A hearty breakfast sets one up for the day, and cats are no exception to this rule. During the course of some 12 hours, a cat will do masses of different things, many of which will require stamina and energy. Although young cats and kittens will require feeding three times a day, most adults will manage happily on two meals. If they are hunters catching their own food, one meal may be sufficient.

cruel to one. He seemed quite grateful that his new neighbor was happy to take on the responsibility of another feline.

Although the kennel was to remain his outside, nighttime accommodation, during the day he led his own, and most natural, lifestyle. He no longer had to hunt for food, as he was fed every morning and evening. He would always be at the back door first thing in the morning, and then at the gate in the evening to welcome his new "human!"

Unexpectedly, she was called away on business for three days, and asked if I would stay at her house, as one of the Siamese was due to have kittens and might need a helping "paw!" (Cautionary note: she had arranged for a "cat feeder" to come in twice a day, but the young lady was not particularly well versed in feline obstetrics, so that is where I came in! Cats cannot be left alone for as long as three days without adequate provision made for their feeding and litter tray cleaning.) Of course I obliged, and had the added considerable interest of observing the "outside cat" as well.

Cats are most fastidious creatures and will always wash after a meal. Many stages are involved in the washing process. Paws are employed as a kind of feline face cloth, used to reach the places that the tongue alone cannot. Post-prandial washing usually starts with the face and head, as the picture shows. This will continue, still using the paws, to cover the back of the neck and ears. The rest of the grooming process can be managed successfully with the sole use of the cat's raspy "designer" tongue; has there ever been a grooming tool better designed for the purpose?

Ablutions completed, a full tummy, and cat is ready for the day. A stroll round the "estate" now ensues, and the cat decides to survey his territory from a high vantage point, i.e. one of the many trees. He stays here for half an hour or so, perhaps to try and decide his course of action for the rest of the day.

The garden was very large, and backed onto a small river. There was a mature orchard with all kinds of trees, shrubs, bushes, and all manner of things to interest a cat. Not only all of this, but there was a cat-loving gardener too, who would give him a little tickle, play with him, and generally show interest!

He was fascinated by the river, and seemed to spend hours just staring vacantly at the rippling water. He must have been able to see things that humans can't, as cats never waste their time; every moment has a purpose. Perhaps his eyesight allowed him to see fish that I couldn't. Who knows? The mystique of the cat is unique to this species. Anyway – the river bank provided a place to ponder, and indeed for a quick scratch!

In the warm summer months a wall is a perfect place for a
cat to settle on, as the bricks or stones will retain their heat.
At this point, the cat was transfixed in bird watching, and
found the wall an excellent vantage point.

It was a long, hot summer so he quite often found himself a
nice cool place for a snooze, well out of the direct sun. Cats
are really most sensible creatures, and one like this, with a
pale coat, is quite liable to sunburn if not sheltered. Again,
the cat knows best! When the weather was inclement, he
would still return to his dog kennel, but this was a very
warm summer.

The final picture shows him at sunset, retiring to a comfortable place under one of the shrubs.

A day in the life of a cat leading a quite natural life. Sadly, after his lovely summer in his ''new'' home, he developed throat cancer and had to be put down. What a year he had, and what insight in deciding to take up residence with this cat-loving person.

More recently, she has had a conservatory added to her house. Where he used to sleep outside is now part of this area, and she proudly hangs a picture of him, in what was his favorite place, in this room. She will never forget him, and I doubt that he will ever forget her and the lovely time he spent for the last year of his life.

CATS IN THE KITCHEN

The heart of any home is surely the kitchen, a place where, in this hectic life we lead today, the family can meet up – even if it is only over the breakfast table! The Victorian kitchen sums up the home-loving atmosphere of this room, a roaring fire, warm cooking range, and the lingering smell of good things being cooked – surely something to tempt any cat. In our modern lives, with clinically clean work surfaces, self-clean ovens, microwaves, and all the paraphernalia that modern technology can bring, the kitchen still

The oven and hot plate provide lovely warm places for a cat, but take care! Do not leave pans unattended. The lingering aroma of a tasty meal will be sure to tempt the cat, and can result in dire consequences for both you and your pet. I know, it has happened to me, but fortunately with no damage to the cats, only to my "gourmet" meal. I was cooking a rather nice veal dish, when some unexpected friends rang the doorbell. As there was at least half an hour before my dinner guests were expected, I invited them in for a drink. Cats had been banished from the kitchen but, unbeknown to me, they managed to slip back in while I was serving the drinks. Result: four avocados minus their shrimps, four veal escalopes missing (but the mushroom sauce was still in the pan), five very happy cats, and me making an emergency telephone call to the local take-out! It seemed amusing, and annoying, at the time, but you can't blame the cats. It was my fault for being careless. It could have ended very differently: the cats could have knocked the pan off the stove, scalded themselves, or even been burned on the simmering hot plate. The results could have been horrendous, but were thankfully minimal, apart from the damage to my purse!

remains the hub of home-life – and the cat still seems to realize that this is the place to be if a tempting tidbit is to be found. It is most often the room where the cat is actually fed, and indeed where he or she will find human companionship.

There are so many interesting things going on in the kitchen, it could almost be considered a playroom for cats; however, there are drawbacks, as most modern equipment can be dangerous. Care must be taken to avoid accidents unless the cat is completely banished from this room.

These really do seem to be "the cats that got the cream!" The cats are seated on the tumble dryer, but note that the door is closed and thus inaccessible to them. Kitchen equipment can be dangerous. Cats seem completely intrigued by washing machines; perhaps they feel that they are a type of television. They certainly seem to enjoy watching the laundry just as much as watching certain programs on the television. Please ensure that you do a "head count" of your feline family before switching washers or dryers on.

To some cats, the sound of water is intriguing, and a dripping kitchen tap will provide an incentive to investigate. Again, there can be dangers. These pictures show adult cats playing with the kitchen sink, and amusing themselves with the soap suds, but if this were a kitten in the same situation, the outcome could be quite different. It is almost unheard of for an adult cat to drown in such a small space but, with a little kitten . . . all sorts of eventualities could occur, and some fatal.

This cat was trying to jump from one work surface to
another, but it didn't quite work out the way he thought.
On the left-hand side the hanging apron has caused him to
skid off direction, and he now seems to be heading straight
into the garbage bin, rather than his intended arrival on the
right-hand work surface! Even simple things like this can be
hazardous to a cat.

This little kitten is happily playing with a leaf from a bunch
of flowers. A pretty picture – but could there be a danger
here? The kitten is near to the stove, but warnings enough
have been given already regarding this piece of equipment.
Many plants contain poisons that are dangerous, some even
fatal, to felines.

Cats love kitchens and, more often than not, are encouraged to this room for feeding. At the same time, this is the area where you prepare your own meals and, to many people, feeding a cat here seems a somewhat unhygienic practice. Cats walk over the nice clean work surfaces and, if they are fed on the floor, provide the possibility of your tripping over their food bowls – you just can't win, can you? It does seem more sensible, and less liable to cause an accident, to feed the cat/s above floor level, but please be careful regarding the disinfectants and cleaners that may be used. Certain chemicals, such as phenols and creosols, can be lethal to cats and will most certainly cause a severe tummy upset at least. Cats also can absorb such poisons through their paw pads, as well as by ingestion. After eating, cats will always wash themselves thoroughly, doubling their chances of being poisoned if such disinfectants are employed.

Tables provide yet another of the "high" surfaces that cats just love to jump onto – and off again – and are most often located in the kitchen area! Cats have amazing powers of elevation, provided the landing surface is non-slip; in the same way, they can "take off" quite successfully if they get a good grip, otherwise anything might happen. To prevent accidents, either to your cat or to whatever happens to be be standing on the table, avoid using a tablecloth, unless it has a non-slip mat underneath it. The vase containing a bunch of flowers would be likely to end up smashed on the floor, and the cat leaping off the table is quite likely to skid and harm herself (not to mention leaving scratch marks on the table).

STEALING FOOD

Cats are born survivors, and are certainly not averse to playing the part of the "cat burglar" when it comes to food. Anything forbidden is an obvious temptation, and probably stems from the cat's natural inclination to stalk and hunt. Why else would a well-fed domestic pet still feel the need to steal from the table? Perhaps to show humans how superior the feline is; a kind of "you are not paying attention, so I'll just grab that piece of meat from your plate and you won't even notice" attitude.

Some cats steal the strangest types of food, and this could be a simple case of the cat knowing best. The pictures here show a cat stealing a cheese cracker; perhaps she knew something her owners didn't, and her diet was lacking in fiber. There again, it could simply be put down to a case of what most cat-lovers refer to as the "perverse law of the cat:" anything forbidden is more

The first principle in any good theft is to case the joint. Cat, realizing the dining room has been vacated of humans, jumps on the chair to see what there is of interest. At this point in the meal, only the cheese crackers remain on the table.

As nothing more tempting is in evidence, cat decides that it may as well try out this feeble offering. A quick look round to make sure nobody has returned to the room, and in an instant the cracker has been commandeered. When a cat is usually fed in its own

bowl, it will be happy to consume its meal from this receptacle; stolen food, however, is a case for special treatment, and will be taken off to some quiet corner to be consumed, much in the same way as a natural kill would be enjoyed.

desirable and will be taken anyway! The type of foods that cats might steal varies tremendously – roast potatoes, raw green beans, and even chocolate. On the other hand, offer the cat the food that it has stolen, and you will be presented with an expression of great disdain!

Pregnant cats, like their human counterparts, are not immune to "cravings" for the most unlikely foods. Ridiculous examples that spring to mind are avocado, Chinese mushrooms, and pickles. One particular very heavily pregnant cat totally disgraced her owners by landing in the middle of a dinner guest's plate, which contained her current preferred food – spaghetti bolognese! Fortunately the guest was a cat-lover.

For whatever reasons, cats, even the best fed, still feel this natural desire for forbidden fruit. The stealth, intelligence, and guile in the way they execute the operation has to be admired!

Having consumed the evidence, the cat returns for more. The plate is now empty, so just where did that cracker come from? Another reconnaissance around the table reveals a large container. What could be in this? In no time at all, the cat realizes that this is the cracker barrel, and now has the difficult decision as to which type of cracker to choose – but she had better be quick before her owner returns to clear the table!

THE CARRIER BAG CAT

Domestic cats that are allowed a "free-range" lifestyle will usually amuse themselves within the garden and surrounding area. However, many cats now find themselves confined to an apartment with no access to the outside world. This, in itself, is not cruel if the cat has never known the fun of the great outdoors; it's more a case of what it's never known it won't miss! Conversely, most cat lovers agree that it is not a kindness to confine a cat that has been used to having a garden to play in to an enclosed, indoor lifestyle. With today's high-rise developments and urban sprawl, many of us have no alternative but to adapt to living in an apartment and, if we wish to share our homes and lives with feline companionship, then so must our cats.

Unless there is somebody at home for most of the time, it is inadvisable to have only one cat. Cats do get bored when left on their own for any great length of time, and another little feline friend can make all the difference between a happy, contented cat and a lonely miserable one. Bored cats tend to be destructive, become possessive of their owners, and, occasionally,

The bag is investigated. This is a lengthy procedure as it is examined, first from a distance, then more and more closely. Not only is it carefully watched for any movement (there could be something ALIVE in there!), it is sniffed to make sure that there is no trace of another cat's smell, and sometimes prodded with a cautious paw.

Closer examination is now required. Balancing on its back legs, the cat cautiously peers into the bag. This will often be done from several angles just to be completely sure that there is no life-threatening monster lurking inside – even a very small one!

turn vicious. A contented cat will, with a little luck, have had so much to occupy itself with all day that it will spare clawing your furniture, shredding the drapes, and knocking over the house plants, and will give you a happy, purring welcome when you return from work.

Confined cats need mental and physical stimulation, and this has to be provided by way of toys. A local pet store will offer a cornucopia of devices designed to keep your cat amused; many of which maybe quite expensive and, to be honest, unnecessary. Often it is the simplest of things that will amuse, and that the cat will not tire of too quickly. Have you never noticed how cats love Christmas time? This is less for the beautiful, new catnip mouse, more for the paper, tags, and ribbons in which it was wrapped! Popular homemade toys include scrunched up balls of paper, pieces of string or wool, cardboard boxes and paper bags (remember a cat could suffocate in a plastic bag). One large, tough paper bag can provide endless hours of amusement to a cat . . . and the game is even more fun if there are two cats participating!

Now satisfied, the cat pulls the bag over on its side for ease of entry. Cats may seem lazy, but they are really only conserving their energy. Why on earth bother to jump into a bag, when it is far more energy-efficient to pat it with a paw and walk straight in? It certainly makes sense to the cat!

The game can really begin! The bag is down, and the cat can get in and out easily. Usually, having got in, the cat will try to "punch" its way out. This is a great game, and can be made even more interesting if a human gently flicks a finger at the back of the bag. It is even better to throw a rolled-up piece of silver paper into the bag too! It makes a splended noise, and the cat will think that there really is something to attack in the bag!

To a small creature such as a cat, this large door secured by a bolt several inches taller than his fully-stretched body may seem like an insurmountable problem. This proves not to be the case. Having examined the door from several angles, the cat realizes that there is no way he can reach the bolt from floor level.

The cat discovers that the bolt is accessible if he stands on one of the work surfaces. From this vantage point he has secure footing for his hind legs.

The grass may be greener the other side of the fence, as the old saying goes, but in cat parlance it would be more applicable to say there is always something more interesting the other side of the door! What we may think is a safely closed door can be a simple exit route for a cat. Any door that only closes by way of knob, handle, or bolt is quite easily opened by a clever cat. Knobs are the most difficult, as the cat has to jump at the knob, turning it at the same time, and swinging his body to pull the door open. Handles, however, are no problem! Jump up, pull the handle down, swing, and – bingo – open door! The obvious solution to this drafty inconvenience is to install your handles upside down.

There are many serious reasons why what lurks the other side of the door should be kept away from a cat. Outside doors may give access to a busy and dangerous road; equally, they could allow a confrontation with the next-door dog.

Even within the home there may be certain rooms that are forbidden to your cat. For example, homes that are secured with burglar alarms linked with pressure pads are not conducive to cats, as the slightest movement will set off the alarm. Any room containing a substance dangerous to cats should be treated with the same caution. Any owner of a home computer or word processor might also consider making the computer room out of bound to cats – they do love playing with the keyboard and sleeping on the warm monitor!

This was the easy part! With nothing to restrain it, the cat simply pushed the top stable door open, balanced on the ledge, and jumped down to the freedom of his garden.

CATS ON HIGH

Whenever possible, cats like to perch as high up as they can possibly manage, but why? They are renowned as the greatest exponents of the high jump, but their ability to leap to high places probably evolved as a way to escape non-arboreal predators. So why should they continue to do this in a safe domestic environment?

They may feel that they need the exercise and that a good leap is the equivalent to a workout at the gym. Hot air rises, so the higher up you are, the warmer you will be; cats do like to be in the warmest places, and they do not need a degree in physics to locate the hot spots in the house. Perhaps they simply do it for fun, or to demonstrate their perverse sense of feline humor. Most cats like to walk along the mantelpiece, and the fact that they usually manage to knock the ornaments off is, in their eyes, not their fault but

The top of the tall Welsh dresser was the favorite summit for this cat. Whenever she was missing, it was always here that she was found. Of course it is possible that she simply thought that this was a nice, safe place from which to view the comings and goings of the household, but she probably had much better reasons to seek refuge here. There were two young children in the house and, much though she enjoyed playing with them, there were times when she simply wanted to rest quietly on her own. Although she was a devoted mother to her kittens, there comes a time when a litter of six boisterous eight-week-old babies gets a little too much to handle. At that age, they seem to want to play 24 hours a day, so who could blame her for seeking her own peaceful corner in a place the kittens could not reach? They might well be active, but they were just not big enough to leap so high! At other times, when the kittens had gone to new homes, she used to play a kind of "hide and seek" with the other feline members of the household and when they found her, they would all curl up together!

yours. What a silly place to put such things when you should have known that the cat would want to walk along there! The same goes for the bookcase; your cat may not be planning his next voyage around the world, but that doesn't mean that he shouldn't knock the atlas down in order to have a closer inspection.

Another favorite is to jump up onto the top of an open door. The cat will happily sit there for any length of time until something of interest, such as a passing human, walks by; he will then launch himself at full power, and leap down onto the poor unsuspecting person! This trick is particularly effective in the bedroom, and an excellent way to awake a human who is late serving the cat's breakfast; even a small cat appears to be very heavy when he lands on you from the top of the bedroom door!

Exposed rafters make for the ideal cat assault course, the most exciting part being actually getting up there in the first place! Thereafter, other games, such as ''walking the plank,'' can be played; this is much more fun for two cats, with one making the other walk across the narrow beam! Cats have an exceptional sense of balance, and rarely fall, but even if one does, it invariably lands on all four paws.

A perfect place for a snooze! A small shelf unit in the kitchen, only a short jump from the work surface and bathed in the sun from a south-facing window, provides a delightful warm area in which to relax and sunbathe. The cat can happily sleep through the sound of the washing machine and other such kitchen noises, but opens a slightly cautious eye as someone enters the room.

Stairs, especially open-plan ones, provide great places from which to view the ground floor of the home and assess what activities are going on. Staircases are also a very good location for hitting any passer-by on the head! In a multi-cat household, the stairs will also provide a great source of amusement; cats may seem to be small, dainty, elegant creatures but two or three hurtling up the stairs at full pelt will probably sound to you (and your neighbors) more like a herd of elephants! Quite often, one can spot the ''pecking order'' of the feline family when they play together on the stairs, as the dominant cat will usually assume the superior position at the top of the flight.

The floor level, in many houses, can be a drafty area, and so many cats will seek a raised place on which to sleep. If you didn't think to place their own bed in such an area, the solution in the cats' eyes is perfectly simple – your own bed will do very nicely, thank you very much! In the same way, cats will prefer to snooze on your chairs or sofa, as both provide a draft-free zone. One word of warning: once your cat has established his preference for your bed as his sleeping quarters, it will be a very hard habit to break, and you will probably end up with a feline bedfellow for life!

CONTRARY CATS

Cats often seem to want to get into the most unexpected, even unwelcoming, places and sometimes go to sleep there too! What on earth makes them do it? No matter how luxurious the cat bed that you provide, your fickle feline will doubtless find somewhere else to sleep. A nice warm place, such as an airing cupboard or a cozy drawer full of soft clothes might seem an obvious choice for a comfort-loving cat, but this is not always the case. One of mine even managed to spend the night in a drawer full of slide mounts in my office; goodness knows why, as there was a perfectly good, warm bed upstairs! When it comes to their sleeping arrangements, cats certainly can be quite contrary.

Many homes have a laundry basket and, given the chance, your cat will want to make this a nest. However, when selecting your basket, do think of the type your cat might prefer! Plastic ones are not really very interesting, as it is difficult for the cat to get his claws into it. A natural material, such as basket weave, rush, or wicker is much more fun, and provides a scratching post for exercising the claws. If you really want to spoil your cat's enjoyment, and save having your laundry mixed up with bits of cane and rush (it doesn't do the washing machine much good either!), then opt for the plastic variety; it will also save your having constantly to vacuum the bathroom floor to remove the debris!

How any cat can sleep peacefully in the middle of a busy office is difficult to understand, but this is this cat's chosen and preferred sleeping place! He appears oblivious to the noise going on around him; printers, fax machines, telephones, and typewriters may all be whirring nearby, but he continues snoozing. The secretaries, realizing that the cat had chosen the desk as his bed, decided that his bedding might as well be put there too! It may look a little strange, but I cannot think of a nicer working environment than one with a resident cat!

Do cats know when their owners are about to go away on vacation? Even an empty open suitcase will be interesting, but one full of clothes is irresistible! Your cat will thoroughly investigate it, rubbing around to leave its own subtle scent as if it is saying, "If you are going away, I'm going to make sure that any cats you meet know that I am here waiting for you to come back home!" Do check a full suitcase before shutting it; it is not impossible for a cat to bed itself down comfortably, and out of sight, within the case. This could have dire consequences; your clothes may well be replaceable, but your cat is not.

THE GREAT OUTDOORS

If you are fortunate enough to have a garden, then you will be able to share the pleasure and enjoyment that your cat will derive from being allowed access to the "Great Outdoors." Even if your "estate" is little more than the size of a pocket handkerchief, your cat will still find many things to explore and discover. However, as with any new experience, it is best to take things gently, proceeding with one step at a time.

You may recently have adopted a cat or a kitten; alternatively, you and your cat may have moved house, but whatever the reason, introducing a cat to the new experience of a garden should be treated with a certain amount of caution. It is most important that the cat should explore the house first and make itself at home. A young kitten will accept its new home very quickly, but an older cat or one that has moved house with you may take considerably longer.

It is no myth that cats will try and make their way back to their old homes, and some have even been known to travel the breadth of the United States in order to accomplish this. Why they have this urge is difficult to say, but there is a possible explanation. Few people buy a "new" house the way that they buy a new car. Houses do not have the same built-in obsolescence as the automobile, and last many centuries. Indeed, many people prefer an older house with a bit of character to it anyway. But what about the cat?

The highly developed feline sense of smell will give a cat a field day sniffing out the new home. There may even have been a resident feline in the house before. This will all have to be investigated before the cat realizes that this is *his* new home as well as yours. As if the trauma of moving isn't enough, the poor cat now has to stake his claim to this new territory as well, and he probably thinks that it would just be so much easier to return to the place that he knew so well, with the old familiar smells to it.

So, do keep your cat indoors for several days (a week or two is even better, if practicable), until he is quite sure of his new home. When he knows where his food bowl and water are and where his bed (or your bed) is, and is generally well settled in, you can start to introduce him to the garden.

At first, allow him out only under your supervision. Even if you are eventually going to install a cat flap to allow him unlimited access to and from the garden, it is important, at this early stage, to let him discover the garden a little at a time. If the garden is very large, you may feel it prudent to separate a "cat sized" area so that your cat cannot get lost. Try to fence off any area that gives direct access to the front of the house and therefore to the road; even a quiet road can be dangerous, as the cat will become complacent, and not realize the danger that the occasional car might bring – maybe until it's too late. Cats that live near busy roads and highways tend to become "street wise" and avoid them, but a cat in a quiet street will never have had to learn the hard fact that a car can be a lethal weapon.

It is not unheard of for cats to be stolen, although it is unlikely that the "cat burglar" would be so bold as to enter your own back yard. However, a cat taking an evening stroll down the road is quite another matter – another good reason for keeping the cat confined to an area

Wisteria is an interesting and colorful addition to any garden and, for a kitten, makes an ideal way to learn the finer points of tree climbing. The lower parts are very sturdy, and provide interesting branches to climb, only one or two feet from the ground. It is usually pruned well back, encouraging strong growth at lower levels, and providing the kitten with an excellent opportunity to try out his climbing skills on the "nursery slopes."

where you can keep an eye on him. Compromise is perhaps the best solution; allow the cat into the garden only when you are there too, and always make sure that the cat is back safely indoors before nightfall.

Caution should be exercised if the garden contains a pond, lake, stream, or swimming pool. Cats can actually swim quite well, but, should one accidentally fall into water, it is quite likely to panic and will need to be rescued. In order to prevent any accident, it is best to ensure that cats do not have access to such areas.

Once your cat has asserted his right to the garden (and this includes leaving little chemical messages to the local cat population that he has taken up residence and, thus, this garden is now *his* territory), there are few other dangers to worry about with a couple of exceptions. Cats will eat grass as a natural emetic, but they are not averse to nibbling away at other plants too; some garden plants, shrubs, and trees are highly poisonous to cats and so should not be planted. The instructions accompanying all fertilizers, weedkillers, slug pellets, and insecticidal sprays, and anti-freeze should be read carefully; these may contain chemicals harmful to cats.

Now, having either removed or neutralized any dangers that may lurk in the garden, both you and your cat should be able to pass many hours together in this pleasantest of environments.

Relaxed and contented, this cat sums up the sheer pleasure of having a garden to relax in on a hot summer's day. The cool grass beneath, and the warm sun on his back, what more could any cat want?

At three to four weeks old, kittens will begin to explore the area outside their nest and away from the caring attention of their mother. Although there are many dangers inside the home, far more lurk in the garden. Young kittens should be supervised as much as possible within the home, but it is imperative that they should not be let into the garden without their human.

Curiosity is inbuilt in cats. This, combined with the urge to explore anything and everything in the newly discovered garden, could lead to dire consequences. The way up is relatively easy, and the main problem arises when the kitten has reached the top of the tree. Having mastered the ascent, how does it get down?

The descent is a tricky business, as this picture shows. On the ground, the kitten appears well co-ordinated and balanced. This was also evident in the way it climbed, albeit cautiously, up the tree. However, although tree climbing is natural to a cat, this young kitten will have to learn the finer points of climbing down. Its first attempt looks like a bad case of abseiling which has resulted in the kitten clinging on with one paw. Balance is clearly demonstrated in the way that the hind legs and tail are sticking forward to stop the kitten falling right off the branch.

This young kitten is approximately six weeks old, and its skeletal system is still developing and so quite elastic. It is unusual for a kitten of this age to sustain a fracture if it lands on a soft surface, such as grass, and has fallen only two or three feet. After any fall, a kitten should be taken to a veterinary surgeon for examination in case of internal injury.

Without the helping hand, the kitten would probably have lost its grip and suffered a tumble. The owner was nearby, and so the kitten was returned to *terra firma* none the worse for wear and, perhaps, a little wiser.

As a kitten grows up and learns to cope with the outside world, expertise in tree climbing will be gained through experience and with a little help from mother. This does not mean that the owner should be complacent when the kitten ventures outside during these early months. Perhaps a comparison could be made; would you let a six-year-old child, who has just received his first bicycle, ride out on his own unsupervised?

If your kitten is missing, it is quite likely that it has taken fright. Perhaps a dog barking, a car backfiring, or some other noise or commotion has scared the kitten, and its natural instinct will be to get as far away as possible. The obvious choice is a tree, preferably as high as it can get. If your kitten does get itself into this predicament and cannot get down, you will have to come to the rescue. Do remember though, that a frightened kitten can scratch and that it is advisable to wear thick gloves. In fact, the kitten will feel more secure if you put it in a pillow case or similar soft fabric bag and, equally, this will make it easier for you to climb down the ladder without a small wriggling feline hampering you.

Some years ago, the Fire Department was called out to rescue a kitten in such a situation. After two fruitless hours of cajoling and appealing to the kitten's better nature, the firemen were becoming increasingly desperate. They were happy to allow a local "cat lady" to "meow" under the tree to encourage the small cat to come down. Much to their amazement, it worked.

As we have seen, the art of climbing up a tree poses no real difficulty, it is the coming down that is the hard part. This six-month-old youngster has learned that getting to the top is simple, but is now somewhat apprehensive about starting the descent. She starts crying for attention in the hope that her owner is in earshot and will come to the rescue. After 15 minutes or so, as there is no sign of assistance, the kitten realizes that she must make her own way down.

The first steps are always the hardest, and the kitten cautiously edges forward. The business of climbing down a tree requires both co-ordination and balance, and the kitten is not sure-footed enough to commit herself just yet. Another quick look round to be sure that there is nobody to help her, and she realizes that she has to take the plunge "single pawed."

As the apple tree was not terribly tall, the kitten decides on a forward approach. She gently edges her way down, using her claws to help her grip, until she suddenly realizes that the ground is but a short leap away. A good kick from her two rear legs and she is off. This tree climbing affair is not really as difficult as it looks, once you are safely back on the ground!

In the wild, the cat's coat color and pattern can prove to be a lifesaver, as they camouflage the cat, rendering it nearly invisible to prey. By nature, cats sleep during the day and hunt by night, so it is during the daytime that they are most vulnerable. A look round the local zoo will confirm this; lions are sandy colored to blend in with the barren landscapes they patrol, the tiger's stripes provide ideal cover in a jungle, snow leopards are white, mountain cats such as the lynx are ticked tabbies . . . the list could be endless.

Archeological evidence suggests that the earliest domestic cats were probably ticked tabbies, such as those found in mummified forms in Egypt, their coats bearing a strong resemblance to the modern pedigree Abyssinnian cat. Through genetic engineering, cat breeders have managed to produce cats with coats of almost every imaginable color and pattern. However, if these cats mate at random, it takes only a few generations of natural selection before the "basic" colors of black, tabby, tortoiseshell, and ginger reappear. Even black cats are rarely truly self-black unless they have been specially bred. Look at a non-pedigree black on a very sunny day and you will notice that vestigial tabby markings can be seen in the coat, and that the coat is not the same color at the tip of the hair and the root.

Dappled sunlight filtering through rose bushes gives the cat ideal cover. The cat itself seems to become an optical illusion. Is it really there? Is it just another lump of soil?

Cats are skillful climbers and use trees to great advantage. Trees are of use to cats in two ways: they provide escape from land-bound predators, and also afford the cat a wide view of the surrounding area when it is looking for prey. The brown, red, and creamy colors in the coat mingle well with the shades of bark on the tree, while the green eyes, at a quick glance, could almost be part of the foliage. Result – one invisible cat!

Even in a brighter place in the garden, without the dappled light, the cat is still fairly unnoticeable. A point of interest: all cats have much more sparsely distributed hair immediately above their eyes. This is more obvious in darker colored cats, but is still noticeable in this tortie. In the wild, a cat spends most of its day asleep, saving energy for the night-time hunting expedition. When the cat's eyes are closed, the paler area of sparser hair gives the impression that the eyes are open and that the cat is awake and alert. This is true of all cats, including the larger species such as lions and tigers.

GOING FUNNY IN THE FLOWERBED

Catnip or catmint, *Nepeta cataria*, is an herb cats just go wild for. It comes in several forms; it is an easy plant to grow in your garden, and your cat will delight in both rolling around in it and nibbling at the leaves. It is also available in a dried form or as a powder in much the same way as one buys culinary herbs for the kitchen. For maximum potency, the fresh plant is preferable, but can send your cat "over the top," so be warned! The dried or powdered form is not so strong, and is often used in cats' toys and playthings to give an added attraction. Catmint causes a great increase in salivation, so do not be concerned if you find a

Although only a small patch of catmint has been planted in this garden, it will soon grow. Even so, the few leaves that can be seen here have clearly caught the cat's interest, and in no time at all, she was nibbling away happily.

Apart from its benefits to your cat, the plant itself is most attractive. It spreads easily and quickly to provide good ground cover, and in the summer months is covered in a profusion of small, purple flowers. It is a sturdy perennial that will die down in the winter. Before this happens, why not pick a bundle to dry indoors, so that your cat will then have the benefits of an all-year-round supply? You will see that the cat, having rolled delightedlly around in the clump of catmint, has now made herself a cosy little "nest," and her pleased expression shows a contented animal, oblivious to the cares of the world.

very soggy catmint mouse, a cat with a somewhat soggy face, and, if it has been eating and rolling in the fresh plant in the flower bed outside, quite likely a disgracefully muddy cat as well!

Certainly catnip can produce some quite curious behavioral changes in your cat. For some, it will induce a laconic trance, the cat rolling around in ecstasy, drooling, and dribbling with half-closed eyes. Occasionally, the effect can be similar to a belligerent drunk, ready to take on the world and fight to the end. However, the most usual effect is a happy, loving, purring pet who is completely relaxed and friendly.

"Moderation in all things" is a common adage, and in this picture it would seem that the cat has failed to follow this advice, and the situation could become out of hand! The thwacking tail, unsheathed claws, narrowed eyes, and flattened ears are all sure indicators of aggression and manifestations that the catmint has well and truly taken effect. Fortunately, herbal substances do not cause a hangover, and she won't remember a thing in the morning!

49

THE SOCIAL CAT – OR ANTI-SOCIAL CAT?

A cat makes an ideal pet: beautiful, lithe, intelligent, affectionate but never ingratiating like the dog, clean, and companiable. So why have just one? Two are much more fun, no more trouble, and little more expensive to keep than one, and they will very likely prove to be inseparable friends for the rest of their lives. An added bonus is that the owner feels less guilty about leaving a solitary feline alone all day when he or she is at work, and will also enjoy the well-earned annual vacation more in the full knowledge that the cat is not serving a solitary sentence in the local boarding cattery.

Apart from these obvious benefits, there are other, more serious, reasons for keeping two cats. A solitary cat, left alone all day, will probably revert to its ancestral behavior – sleeping during the day and hunting at night. In a modern domestic environment, this may well result in an evening spent playing "entertaining the cat." This game continues for several hours and usually requires the owner to throw a toy or similar object for the fickle feline to indulge itself in the natural pursuit of the hunt and the fun of the catch. There is no need to ask who tires first! It is not uncommon for the bored cat to continue this game well after his owner has gone to bed, and a soggy toy mouse dumped in one's face in the small hours of the morning is really not the pleasantest of bedfellows. It does little, too, to make the cat the most popular member of the family.

Two cats make a completely different story. The ideal scenario is to acquire a pair of kittens from the same litter. Having known the comfort of each other since birth, they find the introduction to a new home far less daunting a prospect than it would be for one little kitten on its own. The two together will have great fun exploring and investigating all the new environs, sounds, smells, and other experiences, not least of which is their new owner. They will grow up together in constant companionship.

If you own only one cat, you will never have the chance to watch at close hand the wonderful social life of two (or more) cats living in the same home. In many cases, the antics and tricks that they get up to will make you want to switch off the television and watch the cats instead.

When two strange, adult cats meet for the first time, feline protocol must be observed. The first stage is usually an eye-to-eye confrontation. This is almost a case of which cat can out-stare the other. If one loses interest, and the all-important eye contact, it will walk off, and the impending confrontation has come to an end. If this is not the case, stage two will develop. The cats still relentlessly stare at each other, and their hackles rise. Cautiously, the two cats will circle each other, blowing through their nostrils and mouthing feline obscenities. At this point one will usually back off, as cats are not prone to aggression and will commonly fight only if cornered or protecting their young.

Cats are fastidiously clean animals but communal washing plays a much greater role than that of the simple daily ablutions – it serves as a very important social contact. Two cats washing each other have admitted to the fact that they are of the same social rank, and are no threat to each other. Where several cats live in a household together, a kind of pecking order will develop with the top cat ruling the roost over the rest. Smell is an important sense in the feline world, and cats who sleep together and wash each other will smell the same; a strange-smelling cat would be considered a threat.

Sometimes the social washing can become a little over-zealous, resulting in two exceedingly wet cats! Good friends as the two cats shown above are, it is always nice to have a little wash in private without the need for a friend to scrub your back!

Cats lead very complicated social lives, and will leave little "scented" messages for the neighboring cats in several ways. Cats possess scent glands in several parts of their bodies, the secretions from which can rarely be detected by the human nose. The cat, however, has a highly developed olfactory lobe and is, therefore, able to smell things that the humble human can't. The most commonly used of these glands are sited immediately behind and below the ears, and in the area of the cheek and chin. Opposite, a cat is rubbing around the corner of the house. This practice is often seen in various parts of the home, and the cat will put his "mark" on many domestic items in this way: table legs, chairs, sofas, wardrobes, and any article that he can reach with his face. The cat will pay equal attention to any humans of which he is particularly fond; he will rub his face around their ankles and legs, and to a particularly favorite person this honor will be extended to a rubbing round his or her face. So what does this all mean? The message that the cat is leaving is quite simple and easy for any other cat to understand – this is my house, my home, and my human, so keep off! There are other ways that cats communicate with each other through scent, the most unpleasant of which is "spraying."

A cat with hackles raised and tail fluffed up is usually
associated with aggression, but this is not always the
reason. Animals of many species are referred to as "having
the wind up their tails," and this is just as true in the case of
an excited, playful cat enjoying a game among the fallen
leaves. She is purely and simply having fun!

This is a classic picture of an intimidated cat showing great fear – arching its back, billowing up its tail, and ready to take on all-comers. The cat in question was minding its own business, and quietly walking along the roof of a bungalow. In a split second, this peaceful afternoon perambulation almost turned into mayhem; an unexpected visitor arrived with a large dog. Unused to cats, the dog started barking loudly and jumping at the side of the building in an attempt to attack the cat. It is hardly surprising that the cat assumed this very defensive pose.

CATS WATCHING OR WATCHING CATS

Cats have many ways of reflecting their feelings, moods, and thoughts, not just by their expressions but also with a sophisticated form of body language. What may seem to us a simple movement or action, with an obvious purpose, can well have quite a different meaning to a cat. Only by observing the feline race will you gain an insight into their *raison d'être*; through this deeper understanding both you and your cat will enjoy a more rewarding relationship.

This long, cold stare is definitely the cat's way of saying "keep away, I don't know you." There is no sign of aggression, but the message to keep your distance still comes over loud and clear. There is a kind of protocol that is called for when befriending a strange cat, and this can be a lengthy procedure. Cat-lovers will find it hard to believe that there are people who not only actively dislike cats, but will be wantonly cruel to them too, so who can blame the poor cat for being a little distrustful at first?

The first rule is to let the cat approach you; any sudden movement on your behalf will probably send the cat scurrying away as it senses that you could be a possible danger. Stay quiet, still, and wait for the cat to make his approach; he may well appear to ignore you, but he is really only weighing up the situation. You will look less intimidating if you sit rather than stand, as you will be nearer the cat's level. Try exchanging a few pleasantries; most cats prefer to be addressed in their own language and

"brrrrrp,brrrrrp" seems one of the more acceptable ways to start a conversation (when pronounced correctly, it mimics a cat's purr!). If this is not in your vocabulary, try any soft, gentle words without any harsh sounds, and always keep your voice low. You should eventually gain the cat's confidence, and it will approach you. Again, let the cat make the first move, and allow it to sniff you before slowly proffering your hand. When the cat is satisfied that you are a friend, it will most likely gently reach up, allowing its head to touch your hand; this is the sign that you have passed the inspection and been accepted!

Most cats that are brought up in a family environment will fairly readily accept a visiting stranger; such cats are used to humans, and have no cause to fear them. In no time, the resident cat will rub round your legs, purring, as a kind of feline acceptance of your presence and an invitation for you to give a gentle little tickle to the back of its head and ears (something that most cats adore!).

Peeping over a fence, this cat shows no sign of fear, only curiosity and interest. It might be simply surveying the lie of the land on the other side of the fence, or perhaps something particular has caught its attention.

Cats invariably yawn and stretch as soon as they have woken up. It is a ritual that involves every inch of the whole body. Paws are stretched to reveal the claws, followed by the limbs; lying on its back, the cat will stretch out as far as it can go, the head thrown back to allow for the largest of yawns; finally, the cat will roll over, stand up, arch its back, and ripple every muscle.

Stretched out low in the grass, lying completely still except for the tail thwacking in anticipation, eyes alert and transfixed – these are all sure signs that the cat in the top photograph is preparing for an attack. The subject of the cat's attention is something moving, hence the twitching tail; it may be only a fly or butterfly, but might just as easily be prey or even another cat. Unless it grows bored, the cat will shortly follow on with the "stalk, pounce, catch" routine.

The cat in the lower photograph partly hidden behind a bush, has definitely caught sight of something. The alert expression, erect ears, and bristling whiskers are all indications that the cat is in rapt attention of something important. However, she is still sitting upright, so she is clearly not watching something that she is considering hunting or giving chase to.

58

Cats love rolling over, for a variety of reasons. In this instance, it seems that the cat has rolled on its back in order to allow the evening sun gently to warm its tummy. Cats, like birds, enjoy a "dust bath," and will roll around in soil and dust. This is an effective way of giving themselves a "dry shampoo," as the dry earth absorbs any excess oily skin secretions and leaves the fur requiring only a quick shake and lick to return it to pristine condition. The cat has an effective endocrine system, with scent glands situated in many parts of the body; rolling around will cause these glands to emit a scent, imperceptible to humans, but most noticeable to other cats. This is the cat's silent form of communication with other felines. Another reason for rolling is really quite simple; it is an effective way of getting rid of an annoying itch!

Sleeping is one of the cat's favorite occupations, and a well-deserved one, too, as an active cat really does use up a tremendous amount of energy. However, it is interesting to look at the differences in these two pictures and see what they tell us about the cats concerned. The first is typical of a cat that is sleeping but not completely relaxed. It is curled up in a tight ball, with the tail around its head, trying to look as small as possible. Had this been a cool day, this could be construed as an efficient way of conserving body heat, but on a warm summer's evening, this is hardly the case. As with most animals, the abdomen is the most vulnerable part of the anatomy, and this cat has his neatly tucked away out of sight. This is a cat who is not sleeping easy, and has adopted this attitude as protection against possible attack. The second cat, opposite, however, is quite the reverse. He is feeling totally safe and secure in his environment, as his body language clearly shows. Lying fully stretched out on his side, underside exposed and visible for all to see, he obviously has nothing to fear; not even a whisker twitches as he enjoys a deep and peaceful sleep.

Garden Center Cat

Although, today, few cats really work for their living, many are still retained in a working environment. So why do so many proprietors still keep on the services of a cat when there is no longer any work for it to do? Because all cats have had a course in "public relations" in kittenhood, and know just how to persuade people to do all maner of things they wouldn't normally do! Even if you have no intention of buying any plants (you may not even have a garden), it is always pleasant to spend an hour or two walking around a garden center, and if you find a congenial resident cat who enjoys sharing a stroll with you, you might just stay that little bit longer – or even buy something! This particular cat has lived in the garden center nearly all his life and divides his time between the office and the old stable yard; he only patrols the gardens after the center is closed.

Lord of all he surveys! The old stable yard is given over to garden accessories, such as pots, urns, and tables. This area has become part and parcel of the cat's life, and as such is a place where he feels secure. The yard needs no investigating; this is home to him, and a safe place to take a leisurely stroll.

When the sun comes out, the top of the marble table becomes beautifully warm. What nicer place to make oneself comfortable, and perhaps have a little doze? For certain, this area is "out of bounds" to the customers, so he won't be disturbed.

Off for another walk, and the cat takes again his familiar and well-trodden path. This is his home and, preferring only his own company, he knows the times to pick when he is least likely to meet strangers.

Time to return to the warmth of the office, where he has his own cozy bed on one of the secretary's desks. But, perhaps a quick drink before going back home? The bird bath, filled from a morning shower, provides just what is needed after a walk.

63

MOTHER CATS . . . AND MOTHERLY DUTIES

Cats make the most wonderful mothers and take their maternal duties very seriously. It is rare for the male cat to offer any help or assistance during this time, although occasionally he may assume a paternal role. More usually, the mother cat will have to take full responsibility and rear her litter as a single parent family. During the weeks following their birth, she will have very little time for anything other than her kittens.

Kittens are usually born 65 days after conception, but this may vary by a day or two. One or two days before the kittens are born, the mother will start to make a nest. Unless you provide her with a warm box, suitably lined with alternate layers of newspapers and old sheeting, and positioned in a secluded, darkened room in your home, she will probably choose her own location for her nursery. This may not be to your liking, as cats do have the habit of choosing the most inconvenient (to us, not to them!) places, such as your bed, the wardrobe, or even an accessible drawer. If your cat's pregnancy is planned, you will have a good idea of the date that the kittens are due. If at all possible, try to be available around this time, especially if your cat is a maiden. Most cats cope perfectly well on their own, but it is always preferable for you to be present, just in case there are difficulties and you need to summon the vet. If you were not aware of your cat's condition, and now have no idea when the new arrivals are due, watch for her nesting procedure.

Kittens are born with their eyes closed, and their ears folded forward. As soon as the mother has torn open the sac, and nibbled through the umbilical cord, she will proceed to wash the kitten vigorously. Cats have raspy tongues which not only clean the kitten of any amniotic fluid, but also stimulate the kitten's circulation. With a gentle nudge from mother, the blind kitten will find its way to a nipple and immediately start suckling.

If the kittens are born in rapid succession, the mother cat may not have the time to perform all her necessary duties, so be prepared to act as a feline midwife! The umbilical cord can be snipped with a pair of sterilized scissors, about 1 inch from the kitten, and the amniotic sac gently broken open with your fingers; if the mother is too busy to wash the kitten, rub it gently but vigorously with a piece of towel, as this will get the circulation going. A kitten that appears to have difficulty breathing has probably inhaled some of the fluid; grasp the kitten firmly with your thumb and three fingers, using your index finger as a support to the back of the neck. With the kitten's head pointing downward, raise your hand above shoulder level and swing down hard; this will not harm the kitten so long as you have supported its neck, and will express any fluid that has gone down to the lungs. These tasks completed, return the kitten to its mother, making sure that you have got it attached to a vacant nipple.

The mother cat may or may not eat the afterbirths; some cats will eat each one as soon as they have chewed through the umbilical cord, others leave them until the kittening is complete, while some don't seem interested in them at all. In the wild, the afterbirth provides an essential nutritious food source, enabling the mother to stay with her kittens without having to search for her next meal. Although it is not essential for a domestic cat to eat all the afterbirths, it is advisable for her to eat one, as it contains valuable vitamins and minerals.

The mother will want to stay with her kittens for the next week to ten days, when their eyes open, and so she should be provided with regular light meals, and with her litter tray nearby. If, for any reason, your cat is not happy with your choice of location for her kittens, she will have no hesitation in moving them to somewhere of her own choosing. Unless this is very inconvenient, it is best to let her have her own way, as she may become upset and distressed, and you will be keeping a constant vigil to see where the kittens have been moved to!

For the first three weeks or so, the mother will keep the kittens spotlessly clean herself, as they have not yet learned how to groom either themselves or each other. As they are too small to climb out of their box, they are unable to reach the litter tray and so are completely reliant on their mother to clean up after them.

Between a week and ten days after birth, the kittens' eyes will open and their ears assume a more erect position. They will still not be able to do very much. It is important to keep their nest quiet, as they are now able to hear quite well. The mother will leave them for longer periods, but will not stray far away. The slightest noise from them will bring her rushing back to the nest to ensure that all is well.

As they reach four to five weeks old, the kittens will be able to climb out of their nesting box, and will start to explore the immediate vicinity. They will also be ready for weaning, and so need to learn not only how to eat, but also what the litter tray is for. The mother will wash their abdomens vigorously after each meal, to stimulate their bowels, and will then gently place them on the tray. Most kittens do not really need to be "taught" to use the tray as such, but will usually simply follow mother's example and realize what the tray is meant for! Although they are capable of eating solid food, such as chicken or fish, some are lazy and will still return to suckle from their mother. Perhaps they are more intelligent; why go to the bother of chewing and digesting food when it's much less effort to plug into the milk bar?

At six to seven weeks old, the kittens should be fully
weaned, litter trained, and ready to venture further afield.
Despite their new-found independence, it is quite usual for
a kitten to return to mother for a quick suck, although now it
is more for comfort and security rather than nourishment.
Most mother cats will know when to call a day to breast
feeding, and will discourage their kittens from suckling.
However, there is a slight advantage to prolonged feeding,
as a female cat is unlikely to conceive again while still
lactating, although occasionally a pregnancy may occur. If
the litter was unplanned, this is probably a good time to
have a chat with your veterinarian with a view to making an
appointment for her spaying operation.

GROWING UP

A kitten is officially regarded as a cat at less than one year old, and so it has a lot of growing up to do in a very short space of time. Most kittens have learned the essentials of being a cat by the time they are six months old, but may take up to two years to reach their final adult size. For anyone who has had the pleasure of owning a kitten from an early age, these first few months are simply enchanting, as one is allowed a glimpse into the secret world of a small creature growing up, finding its feet, and entering the big wide world. You have to wait 16 years or longer to see a human child emerge as an adult, but the cat crams it all into less than one short year.

At four to five weeks old, the kitten will venture outside, but with a certain amount of reservation. At this age, the kitten has still not developed complete co-ordination, and appears somewhat wobbly on its legs. It will take a few more days before the leg muscles have strengthened sufficiently to bear the kitten's full weight, and so it will adopt a form of semi-crawling gait. The ears are still not fully erect, and the kitten has yet to discover that its tail aids balance and so it looks awkward.

A week or so later, and the kitten is beginning to look much more like a perfect miniature version of the cat it will become. The ears are fully developed and erect; by now, the kitten has realized that it can move its ears toward the direction of any sound, thus making its hearing much more acute and sensitive. The legs are now strong and sturdy, fully supporting the kitten, so making it considerably more agile. It has also learned how to control its tail and found that raising or lowering it is an invaluable aid to balance.

Around this time, the kitten will become more adventurous and try to climb up onto higher places, in this instance a raised flower bed. To a human, this may seem a minor accomplishment, but to the kitten, it is probably the equivalent of reaching the summit of Everest! To achieve this feat, the kitten will have had to co-ordinate all its faculties; strength, muscles, sight, and balance.

As the kitten becomes more self-confident, it will try to explore further afield. This is the time to be extra vigilant as, when the kitten has familiarized itself with the layout of your garden, it is quite likely to want to make an expedition further afield. In its own territory, a kitten of this age is reasonably safe, as both you and the mother cat are nearby, but all sorts of dangers may lurk the other side of the garden fence. Dogs, other cats (and it is not unusual for a strange tom cat to attack a kitten most viciously), and even people (not everyone likes cats) can put the kitten in a potentially dangerous situation.

By the time the kitten is five or six months old, it is self-sufficient, and capable of performing most things that the fully adult cat can. The exception is procreation, but, even so, some more precocious kittens have been known to become mothers at this age! If you have no intention of breeding from your kitten, then it is wise to have it spayed or castrated; there are so many unwanted cats and kittens in the world that it verges on criminal to add to this already saturated population. At this age kittens are perfectly able to climb trees, have learned the basics of hunting, and are ready to assume their adult role.

WORKING CAT

A pet food cash and carry – what could be a more appropriate setting for the working cat? Plenty of attention from the customers, and extra to eat from broken bags of cat chow! Far from working for his living, this cat *relaxes* for his living; the cash and carry stocks all manner of cat beds and bedding, and the obvious place to find him is curled up in one of the luxury, fur lined, cat igloos! Perhaps he is testing the quality.

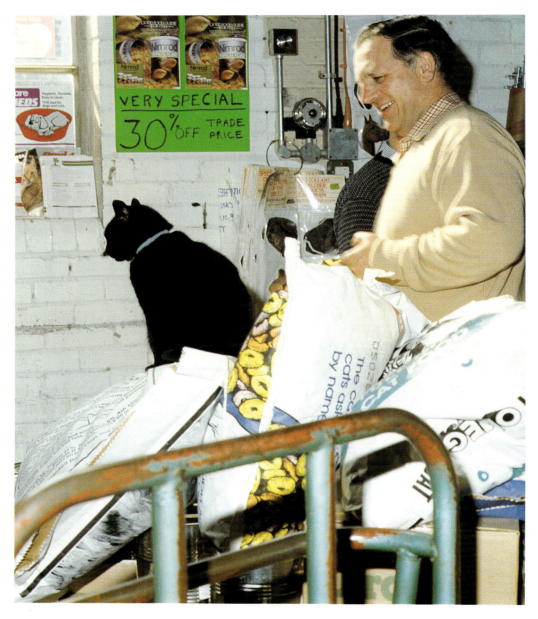

During the course of the working day there are all sorts of interesting activities for the cat to pursue, not least of which is the important task of "keeping the customer satisfied." What more pleasant way of whiling away the time and relieving the tedium at the check-out queue than by having a conversation with the resident cat?

A large warehouse makes for all sorts of interesting things to explore and discover. With goods coming in and going out, day in day out, there is always something new to investigate. To the newcomer to the store, unfamiliar with the cat, it may seem as if he is guarding the stock from theft; so he acts as a deterrent to the light-fingered!

The cat has a quick rub around the trolly, perhaps to check that the customer has bought all that was needed. How could one forget the litter, or a box of toy mice, with the ever-present cat there to remind you of feline needs? A cat can be most persuasive in making you part with your money, and one long, hard stare from the inscrutable eyes will make you wonder if you really have forgotten some vital item that your own cat just could not live without?

HIGH PLACES OUTDOORS

Whether walls, fences, or roofs, cats seem fascinated with high places. Perhaps they are trying to show off their expertise in balancing and their superb ability to leap and climb. More likely, as they are small creatures, they are merely trying to get a better, and higher view of the world around them! An adventurous cat may take on more than it has bargained for when climbing a high rooftop, and suffer the indignity of having to be rescued; there is also a risk of its losing balance and falling, especially in high winds. If your house has guttering, as most do, ensure that the gutters are not blocked. Although the water may only be an inch or two deep, this is still enough to drown a cat, especially one that has been knocked unconscious during a gale.

This cat is the feline clone of the "nosy neighbor." Not content with merely visiting the local gardens, she likes to stare in through the windows to see what is going on; give her the opportunity of an open window, and she is in your house in no time at all. Her daily routine takes her around all the surrounding gardens, until she reaches a high, school wall at the end of the road. At nearly ten feet tall, it is too much for a single leap but the task is swiftly accomplished from one of the dividing fences. From here, she has a panoramic view over most of the locality, and she uses this to her advantage! Safe in her eyrie, she can happily taunt the local cat and dog populations without fear of reprisal, as she knows full well that they cannot reach her. When bored with this game, she is quite happy to spend hours watching the children on the far side of the wall playing in the school yard. Why do the neighbors put up with this behavior? Quite simple – the cat uses a little of her feminine charm! She knows that she is beautiful, with huge eyes that look as if they have been mascaraed, and a coat color and pattern rarely seen in a non-pedigree animal; with all this in her favor, how can she possibly be anything but admired?

A roof is possibly one of the highest places that a cat is able to reach with ease. It may be simple to get up onto the roof, but it is not so easy to get back down. This cat is clearly hesitant and unsure of its next move. From this high vantage point, it searches for an easier way to descend; it gets nearer to the edge of the roof, and looks around to see if there is perhaps some "staging post" it could use rather than making one great leap down. Finally, as there seems to be no alternative, the cat jumps down and lands, without suffering any damage, on all four paws.

A low shed attached to the house once provided an enclosed cat play area, with direct access to and from the family kitchen. Now disused, it still holds an attraction to the resident cats. This one finds it a most convenient place for sunbathing, and even better for bird-watching. However, as the structure was rapidly falling into disrepair, the sensible owners demolished it before any cat could come to harm from the rotting timbers, cracked perspex, and broken chicken wire.

When a fence or wall is only two or three feet from the ground, one wonders what on earth makes a cat want to walk along this route. Surely, the easiest way to get from A to B is to walk along the ground? A cat that has little natural stimuli will probably feel the need for exercise like this that

allows him to practice his balancing skills. In his present
environment, he may not need to be able to navigate a high,
narrow wall, but it is always as well to keep your hand in,
just in case circumstances should change as all three cats
here clearly show.

RESTAURANT CAT

There can be few restaurants that do not have a cat. It is the obvious place for the finicky feline to sample all the best gourmet dishes. It also gives him the opportunity to mingle with the customers and make his suggestions as to what they should choose from the menu; chances are that he has already sampled all the dishes direct from the kitchen, and so has first-hand knowledge of what to recommend! But what does the gourmet cat eat? Canned cat food! This was most definitely his preference, and perhaps he knew that it contained the complete and well-balanced feline diet! Despite this, many restaurant cats do get spoilt by the clientèle; unless the "patron" gives permission, it is best not to feed the resident cat tasty tidbits. He has been fed his proper diet, and really does not need any more. It will only make him unhealthily corpulent and obese.

During the course of the evening, the cat will mingle with the diners, making his formal introductions. It is considered a great honor if he should settle by your table! However, as things begin to get busy, with waitresses scurrying, diners talking and laughing, the cat decides that he is safer off floor level and opts for the safety of the old barrel; at least he won't get his paws or tail trodden on here!

Cats may originally have been domesticated to guard the grain and corn in farmyards, but in our urban environment they have learned to adapt to our ways of life and, where necessary, guard the fine wines in this new habitat! Brought up from the cellar, most bottles will have interesting, musty aroma that just invites any self-respecting cat to come and investigate.

"Just where has the Wine Waiter got to? I've had my dinner and I'd like to order a Cognac!" seems to be what the cat is saying. The "formal" cat dinner is usually served around 6.30 to 7.00pm, before the first customers arrive, and consists of a plate of cat food (preferably two varieties), and a large bowl of water. However, few diners arrive as soon as the restaurant doors open, so the cat has a chance to relax on one of the dining chairs before the evening onslaught!

FANCY CAT!

It is not just "pedigreed" cats that come in many shapes and sizes; the humble crossbreed can be found in as many, or even more, colors, patterns, and fur length! Indeed, pedigree cats are only so because their parentage has been authenticated by one of the many Cat Fancies throughout the world, and so we know exactly what color, what markings, and what length of fur their parents and forbears had. As all cats, pedigree or otherwise, had to start from somewhere before the Cat Fancies organized themselves into the registration of parentage, it is hardly surprising that our ordinary pets come in such a myriad of shapes and sizes – after all, *they* were the ancestors of the noble pedigrees found today!

What color a cat's coat and eyes are depends on the "genotype," or genetic make-up of the particular cat; the way this is manifested, and so

These two kittens are brother and sister. Both are predominantly white, but the female has mainly tortie markings with ginger patches on her head, while the male's markings are mostly tabby. "Blotchy" markings look so very pretty and, given that the white parts are kept in sparkling condition, can make for some of the most attractive cats about!

Ginger cats are often thought to be a male only variety, but this is not always the case. Red is a sex-linked gene, associated with the tortie varieties which are nearly always female, but ginger offspring may be of either sex, although males tend to predominate. It is interesting to note that, like pale-skinned, red-headed humans, the pale nose of a ginger cat is also prone to freckles!

82

how we perceive the cat, is known as the "phenotype." Feline genetics is a very complicated science, and probably one of the reasons why Mendel, the so-called Father of Genetics, stuck to studying sweet peas and fruit flies! Genes come in two basic forms – dominant and recessive – but can be modified by what is termed a "dilute" factor. For example, take two Brown Burmese cats and mate them; brown (more correctly, this is genetically black) is the dominant color and so the kittens should all be brown. If one of the parents carries the recessive gene (blue), then although ALL the kittens will be phenotypically Brown, 50 per cent will also carry the recessive blue gene. If both parents carry the recessive (blue) gene, then there will be a quite different story! In a litter of four kittens, there will theoretically be one Brown, two Browns carrying blue genes, and one Blue; this is known as the Mendelian Ratio 1 : 2 : 1. The dilute factor moderates the coat color, so that Brown becomes Chocolate, and Blue becomes Lilac; add to this the sex-linked genes, that is the red and tortie factors, and everything gets even more complicated.

However, whatever cats have hidden in their genes is not really of interest to most cat owners, as they are concerned with the outward appearance of the cat. And a most sensible approach that is, as working out the probability of what will turn up in the next litter can drive one to the borders of insanity!

So, lets forget science: just admire the many colors of these cats, and enjoy their sheer beauty and elegance! Indeed, if pedigree and non-pedigree cats were to be put in competition together, most pedigrees would be hard put win. Perhaps this is why the Cat Fancies do not allow them to compete against each other!

The tabby is one of the oldest-known cat coat patterns and mimics the coats seen in wild cats. This is a Silver Tabby, but tabbies can also be brown, red or, more recently, blue. The tabby markings can be classic striped, blotched, spotted, or ticked.

The cat opposite is most unusually marked, and it makes one wonder about its ancestry. Blue eyes and a partly restricted coat color make one think that there must be a Siamese lurking somewhere in the background. White tips on the end of its back toes are reminiscent of a Birman

This really lovely, semi-longhaired, tortie-tabby and white, with a pretty face is definitely a female!

Surely this is the classic of cats – a shorthaired, black and white with clearly defined markings and in the peak of condition! Could any pedigree look more aristocratic than this, and doesn't this cat just know it?

HUNTING

Hunting is an instinct natural to all cats, and certainly does not bear any connection with how well they are fed. It is a complete fallacy that only a hungry cat will want to catch mice. Farmers who kept cats as ratters and mousers believed that if they fed the cats, they would become fat, lazy, and completely unable to contain the vermin population in the barns. Nothing could be further from the truth; a well-fed cat will be firm and muscular, with plenty of energy and stamina, and so will make for a much better mouser than its semi-starved and ill-nourished counterpart!

Today, although some are still kept as "working" cats in factories and warehouses, the vast majority luxuriate in the comfort of a warm home without so much as a thought of catching prey to eat. Still the urge to hunt remains; the confined cat will "play hunt" with a toy mouse if it is thrown for it, and watching the way a cat plays provides excellent insight into how the cat would react with the real beast. The cat rarely makes a swift kill; it will watch, crouching low, stalking quietly and softly until ready for the pounce. Then . . . it will play with the mouse, tossing it in the air, catching it in its paws, patting it, and teasing it until the cat becomes bored. It is

The cat has spotted something, and crouches low in the grass to make it as invisible as possible; with ears pricked, whiskers a-quiver, it is just watching and waiting for the right moment. The cat will gently edge forward, still keeping low, and lashing its tail from side to side.

quite possible that many mice suffer their ultimate fate by way of a heart attack, rather than actually being killed by a cat. To many owners, this behavior may seem cruel, but one must always remember that cats are still basically wild animals. Although we have domesticated them in some ways, they still retain much of their wild cat character; this is something that we cannot change nor, in the eyes of most cat-lovers, would want to. Fitting a bell to the cat's collar can sometimes work, as the jangling noise may frighten off some otherwise unsuspecting little creature. In the case of birds, simply do not encourage them into your garden; a well-stocked bird table and other bird food are open invitations to a cat.

A cat that is allowed free-range access to the garden, will often return home with a "trophy" for his unwary owner, and will present it with all due ceremony. The poor cat thinks that it has given you the ultimate honor in presenting you with a nice, fresh vole or bird, and will not understand if you reprimand it for so doing. Quite often, the cat may actually bring you a live animal, in which case try to get it out of the house as soon as possible without the cat noticing – you wouldn't want to hurt your cat's feelings!

Its body still remaining close to the ground, the cat will start to move forward faster, building up to a suitable speed to launch itself for the final part of the sequence, the pounce and kill.

The prey, in this case a field mouse, was in the long grass and was certainly no match for this expert hunter. The pouncing cat, having caught its victim, now holds it down under its right paw. In the wild, the cat would creep off to a quiet corner, away from other animals who might try to steal the catch, and consume the well-deserved meal. The domestic cat will play with it for a while, and finally bring it into his home. That's life.

CATS WITH CHILDREN

Most children are enthralled at the sight of a cute, little kitten, and indeed the two together can make ideal companions – one small being growing up with another, so to speak. However, the decision to adopt a kitten, or even an adult cat, should be made by the whole family. Remember that a cat can live to be 18 or more years old, barring ill-health or accidents, so this decision should not be made lightly. Children can be most persuasive when they want something, particularly at Christmas and birthdays, and will continually pester their parents until they get their own way. How easy it is, when under pressure and busy preparing for the festivities, to say "yes" to almost anything a child requests in order to keep – or just to obtain – the peace!

Toys and other playthings may come and go; what was the highlight of Christmas Day will most likely be rejected and forgotten by New Year, or even earlier. This cannot, indeed MUST NOT, be the case with a live animal, be it kitten, puppy, or any other creature. It cannot be treated like a toy, only to be thrown away when the

It is most important to teach children to handle a cat or kitten with care and respect. It should be gently cradled, with one arm supporting the base of the spine and rear legs and the other holding the cat under the front legs. This little girl has got it right; the kitten feels secure, and so will not struggle to get away.

Cats always know the warmest place, and will more than likely try to get into your bed. It is probably not advisable to let a very small kitten in bed with a child, as children tend to be restless sleepers, and may inadvertently roll over on the kitten. However, an older kitten or adult cat can make a delightful bedtime companion, and a gently, reassuring purr will probably have your child off to sleep in no time at all!

battery has run out, friends visit, or something more amusing comes to light.

If you decide on a feline addition to your family, think carefully about the right time to integrate the new kitten into your home. Any busy time, such as Christmas, is not really suitable. Any young creature, newly removed from the comfort of its mother and siblings, will feel frightened and alone in a new environment for at least the first few days. This introductory period should be a quiet time, allowing you and your family to give the kitten your undivided love and attention when it needs them the most. If the kitten is to be a present for your child, then make alternative arrangements; explain that the kitten will arrive in a week or two and, in the meantime, make a present of a book on kitten and cat care, a picture of the kitten and perhaps its mother, litter tray, feeding bowl, and other paraphernalia that the kitten will need. This way, the child will realize that the promise of a kitten is not an empty one, as you have gone to the expense and bother of buying all the equipment needed!

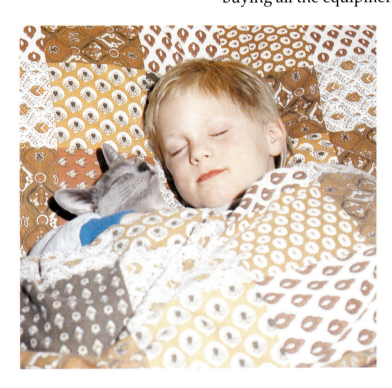

These two have become inseparable friends, and will learn from each other. As the child discovers the pleasure of owning a pet, the cat becomes confident that the child will cause it no harm.

Whatever your age, a cat can make an ideal companion. However, it is well to consider the age of both the cat and the human if the relationship is to be mutually beneficial! In a home with young children, it is better to have a similarly active young cat who will enjoy the childrens' toys and games. For an elderly person, the frenetic activities of a young kitten are probably just too much to cope with and could cause accidents. Kittens are notorious for running around your feet, which might cause a nasty fall. Equally, a kitten could suffer badly if it is trodden on.

Perhaps a good comparison for the suitability of cat to home is as follows. Children love to see their grandparents, but both generations would soon tire if they lived together permanently.

Many cats enjoy helping their owner with the everyday chores and this can include the gardening. As usual, if there is an easy way, the cat will opt for it! Why walk when you can ride?

Some cats just love to get as close as possible to their owners, and they can't get much closer than by curling up around your neck! As they grow bigger, they will usually settle for a perch on your shoulder.

A cat can provide much by way of companionship to a senior citizen. Recent medical research has shown than people who own cats are less at risk from heart attacks and suffer less from stress, too.

Fighting like cat and dog? Not necessarily! Cats and dogs can get along very well together, as long as a little time is spent on the introduction. Meetings should always be supervised at first.

It is always easier to introduce a younger animal to an adult, that is a puppy to a cat or a kitten to a dog, than to integrate two adult animals into the same household. With time, and patience, the latter is also quite possible but will take longer. If the newcomer is the younger, the older animal will usually try and "mother" it. A good method of effecting this type of introduction is to make sure that the two animals smell the same; handle both equally so that they take on your smell! This is even easier if you frequently use a perfume; a very little dab on both cat and dog and they will find, smell-wise, that they are of equal status and, therefore, do not pose a threat to each other.

Another method is the "can be seen and smelled but not touched" approach. Most pet stores will sell kitten/puppy pens. These are plastic-coated, wire containers, usually about 2 feet 6 inches (76 cm) high by 2 feet 6 inches (76 cm) deep, and 4 feet (122 cm) wide, with an openable lid at the top. (Smaller and larger ones are available, but this size is particularly suitable for a cat.) Place the cat in the pen, and allow the dog to look at and sniff it. There will probably be an outburst of hissing and spitting from the cat, especially if it has never encountered a dog

This young English Setter and the family cat are having a great game; it could be called "who's top dog?", or perhaps "I've got you under my paw!" It starts with the cat sitting on top of the chair, batting the dog on its head with one paw, and then the other. Then it's the dog's turn, and the game continues in this vein until one or the other has won – in this case the dog, and the cat assumes a submissive position.

before, and the dog will most likely show a quizzical expression. After a while, swap their positions, so that the dog is confined and the cat "in charge" of the room. Only when you are around to keep an eye on the situation, gradually allow them to roam free in the room.

Generally, the cat will get the better of the dog. Cats are quicker, more lithe and, of course, are the greatest exponents of acrobatics – they can jump their way out of most situations! The cat will usually escape unharmed, leaving the dog nursing both a scratched nose and a severe dent in its pride. One word of warning: some breeds of dog have an inbuilt instinct for chasing and catching prey, in particular many of the terrier

varieties which have been used as "ratters" for centuries. A working, as opposed to a "show" dog of this type will not recognize the difference between a cat and a rat, and so the introduction should be treated with great caution until you are completely sure that the dog no longer poses any sort of threat to the cat.

Once the "ground" rules between cat and dog have been established, they will become great playmates. The cat will let the dog know, in no uncertain terms, if the game is getting too rough. A bit of "rough and tumble" is fun, but there are limits; the cat will hiss at the dog, arch its back, and stalk off as if it were saying, "Those are not the Queensberry rules."

Not, of course, that the cat is a bad loser, but it is definitely giving the impression of "I haven't won, so I'm not playing this game anymore!" Even a gentle nudge from the dog is not having much effect.

Drastic steps are needed now: "If you won't play with me, I'll have to take you by force!" Setters are gun dogs, with soft mouths that never damage the game they retrieve. With his mouth wide open, this dog is very gently maneuvering the cat into a position where he can pick it up, very much in the same way a bitch would with her pups, or a cat with her kittens. This effected, the game can start all over again!

. . . AND BIRDS

As a general rule, keep small birds and cats apart. Even the supposed safety of a cage will not protect a bird from a determined cat. They have even been known to open the cage door, and one rather enterprising feline managed to knock the bird cage onto the floor, pull the removable base out, and release the two birds inside. No damage was done, other than a few missing feathers, but only because the owner was in the same room. Moral: do not leave a caged bird and a cat alone together – you could be attending a small funeral sooner than you would wish.

Although the tallest of any breed of dog, the Irish Wolfhound possesses one of the most delightful temperaments. Living with a feline family of Longhair Chinchillas, this fine animal developed a rather cat-like outlook on life. Although spayed, she was more than happy to help out with the maternal duties, licking and washing the kittens; they, in return, were more than happy to snuggle up next to her for warmth and security.

This unusual relationship developed in a curious way. Included in the household were a pair of canaries. One died, and the other pined for its friend; the children of the house were saddened too. A couple of days later, there was a commotion in the kitchen. The "senior" cat had caught a canary. Far from damaging, or even harming the little bird, he was holding it gently in his mouth, much in the way a mother cat would hold a kitten, with an expression on his face as if to say, "Well, you lost one canary, so I've found you another!"

Another unlikely looking pair, but these two really did get on together! The parrot, a Red Wing Macaw, lived with his owners and their rather large family of cats and kittens. To visitors, he was a rather frightening bird, not averse to barricading you in the bathroom, threatening attack if you dared venture out. Whenever guests came to the home, he was confined to his perch and chain, as he really could attack! However, he possessed a "Jekyll and Hyde" character, and was a completely different creature when left with the cats and kittens. He would gently "peck" the kittens to groom them; if the kittens crept in bed with their owners, he would still continue in this way and, when the ablutions were completed to his satisfaction, would proceed to peck the buttons off his owners' pyjamas! A talking bird, he learned how to sing and hum, and it was not unusual to find him gently crooning "Baa Baa Black Sheep" to the kittens, as if lullaby-ing them to sleep!

Although pedigree cats do not vary in size to the same extent as dogs, there are still many different breeds to choose from and some will certainly grow to be larger than others!

It is a fallacy to think that pedigree cats should be treated like hot-house plants, forever cosseted, needing special diets, and never allowed access to the garden where, heaven forbid, they might even encounter one of the local cats! On the contrary, pedigrees can be just as robust, and have as much stamina as any other domestic feline. They

This Shaded Silver Persian (Longhair) is quite an aristocrat among cats, and is related to the Chinchilla, the cat often seen gracing advertisements in glossy magazines. As with most Persians, they are quiet, companionable cats, but extra attention must be paid to that long fur to keep

them in sparkling condition. Persians (Longhairs) come in so many different colors that it would make far too long a list to name them all, but if this is the type of pedigree cat that you seek, you would be well advised to seek advice from a reliable specialist book.

certainly need no more special attention than that required by their relatives who just happen to have lost their birth certificates!

Any cat will benefit from a sensible, well-balanced diet, and this can be reasonably supplied by many of the proprietary brands of cat food. If fresh food is to be the staple diet, then it will be necessary to add extra vitamins and minerals to keep your cat in the peak of health. It is said that the way one looks reflects what one eats and, in the case of the cat, this could not be more true. A glossy coat free of knots and tangles, lustrous

The Himalayan Persian (Colorpoint Longhair) is a manmade breed derived from an original cross between a Persian and a Siamese. Over the years, breeding programs have been developed to ensure that the true Persian type remains, with only the restricted coat pattern reflecting the Siamese influence. This kitten is a Tortie Point, a female only variety.

The Korat is one of the few natural breeds of cat. It has changed very little since first imported from its native Thailand to the United States in 1959. Paintings of cats, dated circa 1350 – 1767, show the Korat in its characteristic "silver blue" color, the same as it is today. It is an enchanting breed, generally smaller than most other varieties, quiet, intelligent, and with huge green eyes.

Burmese are one of the most popular breeds of cat, and, like the Siamese, come in a variety of colors. Although not as glamorous as the Siamese, they have found their way into people's hearts through their loving disposition and friendly, outgoing nature. But do not be fooled, they are every bit as intelligent as the Siamese, and will get up to just as much mischief, given the chance! They also do not like to be left alone for long, so they should have either a feline friend, or, if this is not possible, an attendant human to share their games and provide companionship.

The Siamese is probably the most instantly recognizable of pedigree cats, and this elegant cat also has the distinguished honor of having gained the "Supreme" title. Siamese are well known for their intelligence, loyalty, and most distinctive voices.

eyes, a lithe, muscular body, bristling whiskers, cold wet nose, and a generally alert expression are all indicative of a healthy animal.

Whether pedigree or otherwise, all cats will benefit from a little assistance with their grooming. A shorthaired cat will enjoy a regular comb and brush, just to help remove the dead fur and prevent fur balls forming in its stomach; follow this up with a polish with a piece of velvet or a soft chamois leather, and you will have a cat ready to grace any cat show. Longhaired varieties

They do like to "talk" to their owners and, being highly sociable creatures, will want to be involved in your every activity. To the aficionado, this is a positive "plus", but not everybody wants a cat that is quite so demanding of their time.

The Russian Blue, as its name suggests, originates from a somewhat cooler climate than that of the Korat. The original name for this breed was the Archangel Cat, as it is believed that this is where they first came from. The Russian has an unusual coat, short and plush to the touch, but concealing a "double" layer to keep out the cold. Their distinctive long legs, elegant posture, and high-held ears ensure that they always have a popular following among cat fanciers.

will need considerably more attention, as they are really unable to look after their luxuriant coats without help from us. They will need to be brushed and combed every day for at least ten minutes in order to stop their coats becoming matted – and matts are rather like rust on a car, once it starts it just spreads. In severe cases, this will result in a trip to the veterinarian to have the matted areas removed under anesthetic. This can easily be prevented by getting both yourself and your cat into a daily routine of grooming.

An annual visit to the veterinarian is imperative for all cats, not just for the booster vaccinations against enteritis and cat 'flu, but also for a general health check-up.

If the Korat is one of the smaller pedigree breeds, then the British Blue must surely be one of the largest. Their sheer size reflects their hearts of gold, as they are most loving and affectionate. As with most breeds, the female is smaller than the male, but, even so, they can grow to be larger than most cats. This male neuter weighs in at almost 18 lbs, and this is not due to obesity; if you like a good-sized cat, this is obviously the breed for you! Their thick, plush fur will need a little extra attention with a daily brush and comb, but other than this, they make quite delightful pets who demand little by way of special attention. British cats are available in as many colors as Persians, so you are certainly spoiled for choice in this direction!

Cornish Rex cats, with their distinctive curly coats and whiskers, are a more unusual breed. The name reflects the region where the first example was discovered, Cornwall in Southwest England. The Rex part refers to the curls in the coat, known as rexing. The Cornish Rex has an "Oriental" look about it, with a long face and large ears. Another similar, but genetically unrelated breed is the Devon Rex, but this is much smaller and does not usually have such a thick curly coat. Rex do not need a tremendous amount of grooming, but do watch out in summer; the sparse fur on their ears means that they can get sunburned, and a little sunblocker cream might well be needed! Interestingly, it would seem that the Rex coat does not cause a reaction in those whose asthma is triggered by an allergy to cat fur, making this a particularly suitable cat for anyone who suffers from this condition. In character, Rex are extremely extrovert and will get up to the most outrageous pranks and games, climbing curtains being a particular favourite!

The Abyssinians (and the Longhaired version, the Somali) have a most unusual "ticked" coat, which gives them an almost wild cat appearance. However, in temperament, nothing could be further from the truth as they are a most loving variety of cat. The Abyssinian first appeared in Britain in the 1800s, and is thought to have originated in Abyssinia (now Ethiopia), traveling to the U.K. by way of merchants' ships. It is certainly a strong possibility that it originally came from this part of the world, as early Egyptian drawings of cats show a marked similarity to the modern day Abyssinian.

These cute little bundles of fur are an eight-week-old litter of Blue-Cream Persian (Longhair) kittens. Even at this age, they are showing signs of the profuse coat that they will eventually develop when fully adult, so the kittens should start being accustomed to their daily grooming routine as soon as possible. The addition of a little baby talcum powder to the coat will give it extra body, but do remember to make sure that it is well brushed out if you are entering your cat in a show (it may be disqualified if any trace of powder is found.) When mature, Blue-Cream Persians (Longhairs) will have deep copper eyes, small neat ears, a distinct ruff around the neck, and a densely plumed tail. As long as you have time for the daily brush and comb, they make wonderful pets with gentle and loving dispositions.

THE SEASONS

If your cat has access to your garden, each season will provide something different to amuse it. However, common sense should prevail when you are undertaking routine gardening assignments. Always keep your cat indoors if you are using a motor mower or other power devices, such as a hedge trimmer or strimmer. Read the instructions on any lawn preparations or weed killers, as some contain chemicals dangerous to cats; although animals may not be mentioned specifically on the label, take it as a rule that any warnings of dangers to children automatically apply equally to pet animals too.

SPRING

Spring is always a time of interest and excitement; the garden starts to come alive after its winter hibernation, birds start nesting, and bees prepare to collect pollen for their honey. If this is an exciting season for us, just think how much more interesting it is to the cat; after months of frosts and snow, the garden will provide much that is new for the cat to explore, not least of which are new smells! Many cats will not venture far in winter, preferring the warmth of their own fireside, but the warm spring sunshine will soon encourage your cat back into the garden. Most cats mark their territory with their scent, but much of this will have been rendered odorless by the winter frost; now is the time for your cat to restate his claim to his territory, and he performs this as a kind of feline ''beating the boundary'' ritual.

For a kitten of this age, Spring itself is not the only new experience; this may well be the kitten's first foray into the great outdoors, and so the whole garden presents scope for major explorations and discoveries. But do take warning: although this little kitten has only managed to climb a few feet into the wisteria, it will not be long before she goes further afield.

SUMMER

This season conjures up the thoughts of lazy, hazy days in which to bask in warm sunshine, and the cat feels just the same! Like us, cats enjoy sunbathing, but, although they do not tan the way that we do, they can still undergo some pigmentation changes. The coats of dark-colored cats will be bleached to some degree by strong sunlight; black cats will take on a browner hue, while brown cats will show a distinct reddish tinge. Pale-colored, shorthaired cats, especially the Rex varieties, can get sunburned ears, noses, and faces if they spend too long in the sun; a little sunblocker will help the situation, but exposure to the sun over a prolonged period may result in permanent freckles! In extremely hot climates, a cat may suffer from heat stroke; with their profuse, long coats, Persians are more susceptible than other breeds. Some owners clip a longhair's coat short during this season, but a simple solution for most overheated cats is to stand them in a bowl of very cold water; this will soon cool the blood, and thus the whole cat. You can give the cat a cold shower but, if you do, remember to rub most of the moisture out of the coat with a towel; it is still possible for the cat to catch a chill if it remains soaking wet for any length of time.

There are all sorts of things in a Summer garden to interest a kitten, but do not let its curiosity get the better of it. An older cat will know the summer scenario, and the dangers it might encounter, but a kitten has yet to gain this experience. The main things to watch out for are wasp and bee stings, and, if you live in more tropical climes, snake bites. As a young kitten will be intrigued by the scent of flowers, and equally interested in exploring any areas of long grass, both of these present a real possibility of injury. Unless the sting is in the mouth or throat (which can cause great difficulty in eating or breathing), you can easily treat it at home. However, it is always worth having a word with your veterinarian, just to be on the safe side. There is little you can do for a wasp sting other than apply a cool compress; a bee sting must be removed before applying a cool compress, and, depending on the type of snake, a visit to the veterinarian may be necessary to treat the bite. Most kittens learn very quickly to keep well out of the way of these creatures, and are more than likely to pass a happy, first Summer without incident!

FALL

Berry-laden trees will encourage many birds, and so arouse
the interest of your cat. Having lived with a resident cat for
the best part of the year, the birds should be well
accustomed to getting out of the way quickly, and so are less
likely to be caught than they would be in the Spring. Some
berries, although nutritious to birds, can be harmful to a cat,
so you would be wise to check a list.

Most cats are intrigued by falling leaves swirling in the wind, and will derive hours of pleasure from chasing them around the garden. As the first frosts approach, the leaves take on an interesting, crunchy texture underfoot, and this seems to amuse cats even more. A cat will play for hours in dead leaves, but be careful when you sweep them up to make a bonfire. Make sure that your cat is kept safely indoors; she is not to know that you intend to burn what she considers a source of amusement, she is quite likely to want to join in too.

WINTER

Many adult cats find snow unpleasant; it does not support
their weight, so they are likely to end up knee deep, it is
very cold, and it makes the coat wet – and cats hate being
wet! For these two kittens, it is a new experience to be
discovered, and they leap into the snow-covered garden as
soon as the door is opened, while their more senior feline
relations watch with some amusement from the window!

Even though the kittens sink up to their shoulders in snow, they still think that this is a great game, and enjoy it even more when flakes start to fall again! Games of hide and seek, catch me if you can, and many others all take on a new dimension when played in the snow. After an hour, when they still showed no signs of wanting to come indoors of their own accord, their owner carried them back in.